CLASSIC

OPTICAL
ILLUSIONS

CLASSIC

OPTICAL
ILLUSIONS

By Gyles Brandreth, Michael A. DiSpezio,
Katherine Joyce, Keith Kay,
Charles H. Paraquin

Main Street
A division of Sterling Publishing Co., Inc.
New York

Material in this collection was adapted from

The Great Book of Optical Illusions © 1985 by Gyles Brandreth
World's Best Optical Illusions © 1987 by Charles H. Paraquin
Astounding Optical Illusions © 1994 by Katherine Joyce
Little Giant Book of Optical Illusions © 1997 by Keith Kay
Visual Thinking Puzzles © 1998 by Michael A. DiSpezio
Little Giant Book of Optical Tricks © 2000 by Keith Kay

10 9 8 7 6 5 4 3 2

© 2003 by Sterling Publishing Co., Inc.
Published by Sterling Publishing Co., Inc.
387 Park Avenue South, New York, NY 10016
Distributed in Canada by Sterling Publishing
c/o Canadian Manda Group, One Atlantic Avenue, Suite 105
Toronto, Ontario, Canada M6K 3E7
Distributed in Great Britain by Chrysalis Books
64 Brewery Road, London N7 9NT, England
Distributed in Australia by Capricorn Link (Australia) Pty. Ltd.
P.O. Box 704, Windsor, NSW 2756, Australia

Printed in China
All rights reserved

Sterling ISBN 1-4027-1064-X

CLASSIC OPTICAL ILLUSIONS

CONTENTS

INTRODUCTION

Not to Disillusion You, But ...

Optical illusions take advantage of basic weaknesses in the visual system. Playing with these illusions helps to sharpen your visual thinking skills. Would you like to know more?

Whenever you "see" an object, light rays are actually reflected from the object, past the protective outer cornea, and through a tiny opening called the pupil. The pupil is the dark spot in the middle of the iris. And the iris is the muscular disk that changes the size of the tiny opening, depending on the brightness of a scene. (The pigments in the iris determine your eye color!)

Behind the pupil and the iris is a lens that is so flexible that you can focus on near and far objects, and even see things that you're not really focusing on. The light rays then pass through your jelly-like eyeball and onto the retina—a screen at the back of your eye. The retina is made up of little cellular structures called rods and cones, which are sensitive to light and color. From there, a pathway called the optic nerve relays the image to the brain.

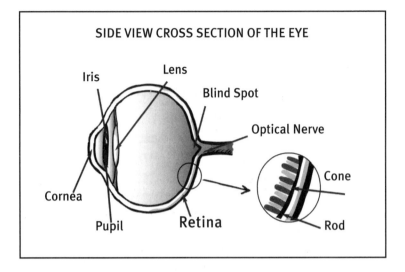

Your brain interprets this information as a picture—ah, but not always "correctly"! There are no light-sensitive cells, where the retina and optic nerve connect, creating a blind spot. And sometimes, the brain simply takes short cuts in processing information.

So, usually we see what we expect to see. But sometimes our perception lets us down, and we perceive something to be so that isn't really so!

That should happen to you quite a few times as you look through this book, because optical illusions very often manage to fool your perception. And then you begin to wonder—*is seeing really believing?!*

౧౧౧

THE LONG
AND THE
SHORT OF IT

BLOCKBUSTER

This white block is a little bigger. . .

. . . than this white block

—isn't it?

Solution: p. 251.

RIGHT ANGLE?

Which is larger:

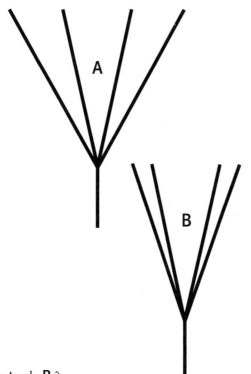

Angle **A** or Angle **B** ?

Solution: p. 251.

A QUESTION OF LINES

Which of the three horizontal lines is the longest: the top one, the middle one, or the bottom line?

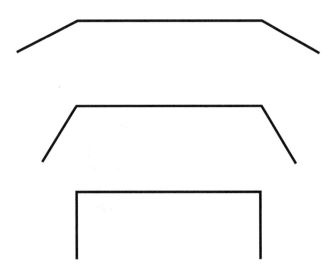

Solution: p. 251.

A QUESTION OF ANGLES

Which is the longer line:

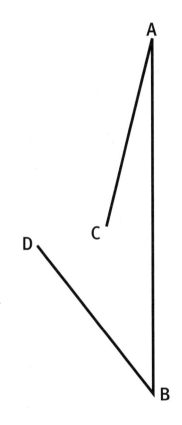

the one from **A** to **C**

or

the one from **B** to **D**?

Solution: p. 251.

HOW FAR THIS TIME?

Is the distance between **A** and **B** greater or smaller than the distance between **C** and **D**?

A
_____

C
_____

B

D
_____

Solution: p. 251.

POINT OF VIEW

Look carefully at the two horizontal lines.

Which one is longer:

the top one or the
bottom one?

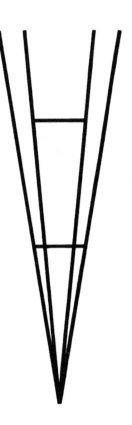

Solution: p. 251.

A CURVE BALL

Which of the three arcs is the biggest:

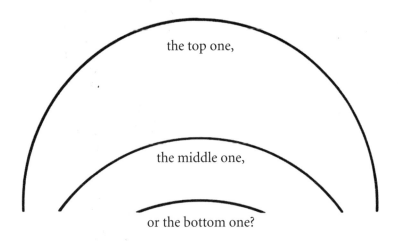

the top one,

the middle one,

or the bottom one?

Solution: p. 252.

FROM HERE TO THERE

Is the line from **A** to **B** longer . . .

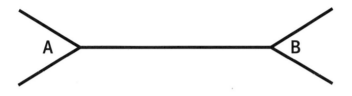

. . . or shorter than the line from **C** to **D**?

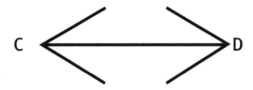

Solution: p. 252.

PARALLEL BARS

Look carefully at the parallelogram below. Which line is longer:

A-B or **A-C**?

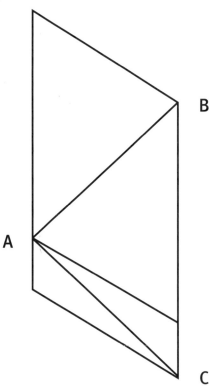

Solution: p. 252.

THICK AND THIN

Of the two thin lines, which is the longer?

Solution: p. 252.

FIDDLESTICKS

Which of the two horizontal lines is the longer? It looks like the top one, but are you sure?

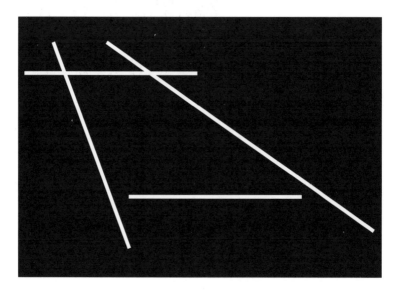

Solution: p. 252.

POPCORN, ANYONE?

Which of these moviegoers is the tallest?

Solution: p. 252.

INVESTIGATE THIS

Each of these detectives obviously enjoys wearing a different. But which detective has the largest mouth?

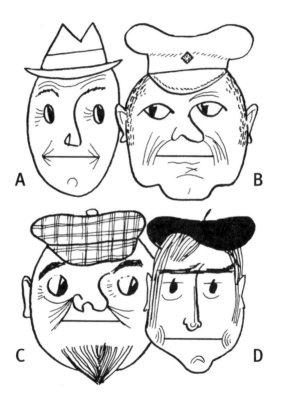

A

B

C

D

Solution: p. 252.

CLIPS AND PINS

Which is the longest object in this picture?

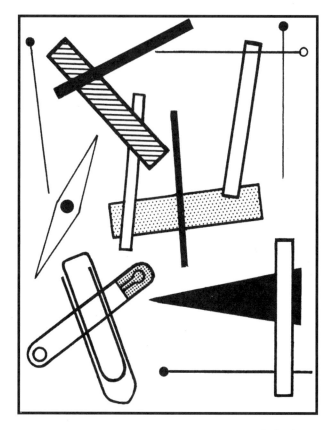

Solution: p. 252.

BLINDED BY THE LIGHT

One window has vertical slats. The other has venetian blinds. Which window is taller ...

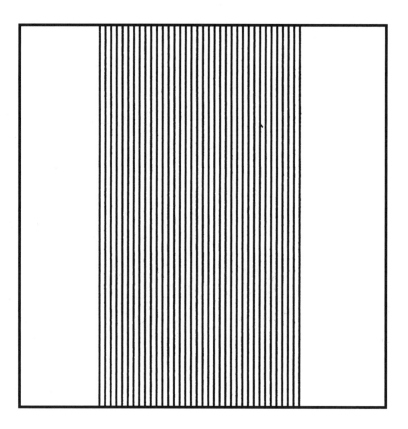

... and which is wider?

Solution: p. 252.

SAWTOOTH

How does height **H** correspond in size with width **W**?

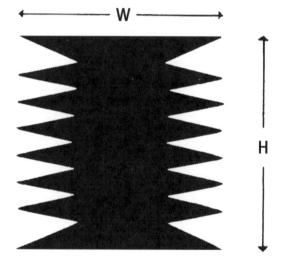

Solution: p. 253.

MAKE YOUR POINT

Is the dot midway between the point and the base of this triangle—
or is it too high up?

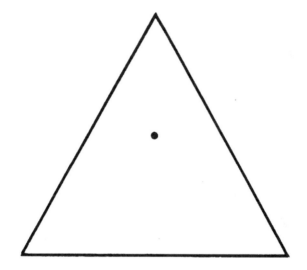

Solution: p. 253.

PAPER AIRPLANES

Are the crossbars exactly in the middle of the center line of these triangles?

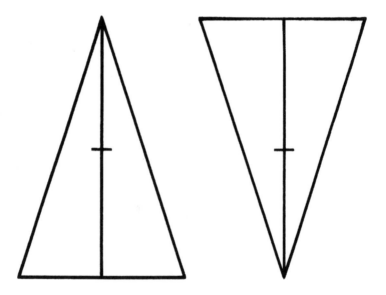

Is **A** larger than **B**?

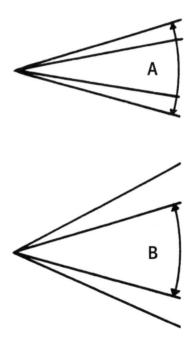

Solutions: 253.

DUMBBELLS

Which lines are the same length?

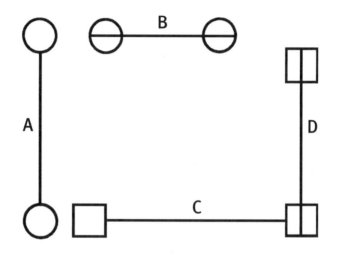

Which is longer, line **A** or line **B**?

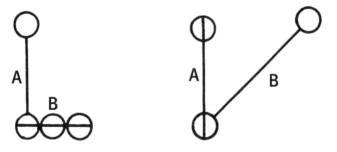

Solution: p. 253.

HIGH HAT

How does the height of this top hat **A-B** compare with the width of its brim **C-D**?

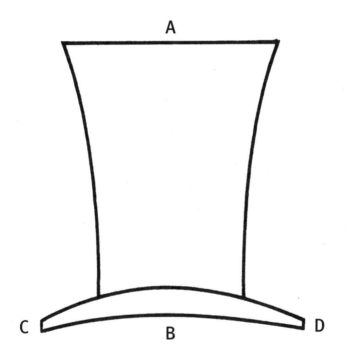

Solution: p. 253.

BELL TOWER

Is the church tower taller than the base of the church is long?

Solution: p. 253.

PASSING LANES

In the left-hand figure, is the diagonal line straight?

In the right-hand figure, which line is the continuation of **A**?

Is it **B**, or is it **C**?

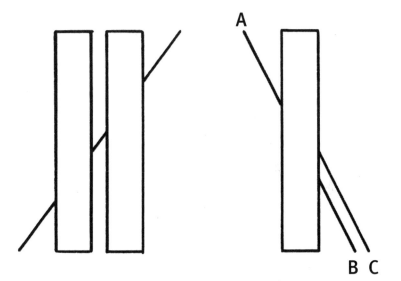

Solution: p. 253.

CENTERFOLDS

Is the center line **A** shorter than ...

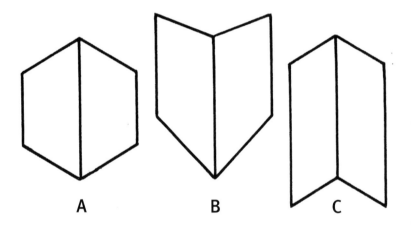

A   B   C

... the other center lines in **B** through **F**?

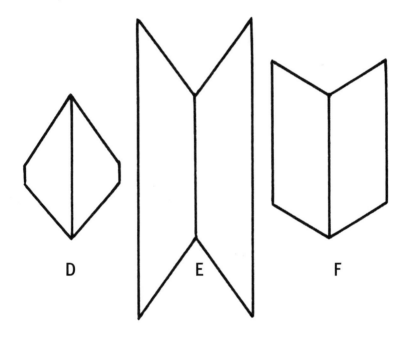

D   E   F

Solution: p. 253.

IN THE ARENA

Are the lined-in sections **B** of the circle larger than the open sections **A**?

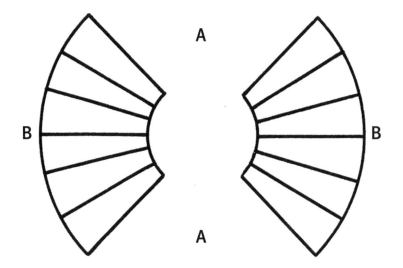

Solution: p. 253.

FLORENCE NIGHTINGALE

Which nurse's hat looks bigger?

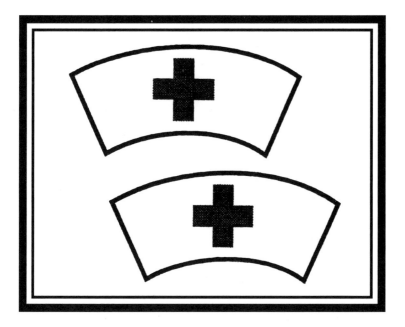

Solution: p. 254.

FISHTALE

Fishermen are always boasting about the size of the fish they have caught. This man has caught two fish. Which one is bigger?

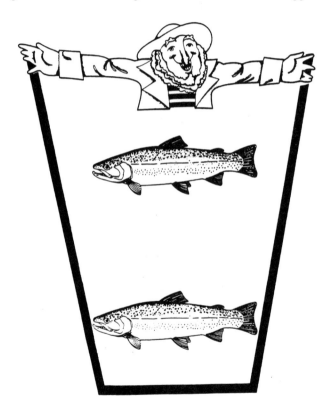

Solution: p. 254.

CHAMELEONS

Which lizard is longer?

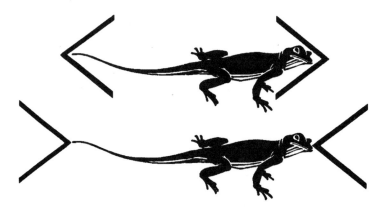

Solution: p. 254.

HIGH DIVE

Which block is bigger?

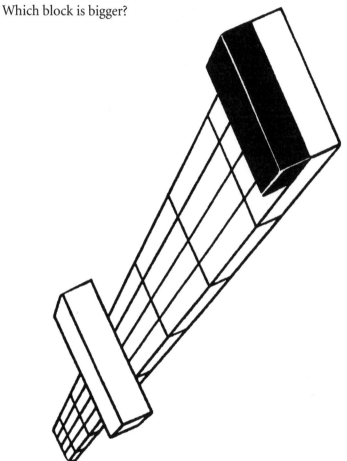

Solution: p. 254.

ZIP YOUR LIP

Which of these two boys has the wider mouth, **A** or **B**?

Solution: p. 254.

COUP DE GRÂCE

Which of these two sabers is the longer, **A** or **B**?

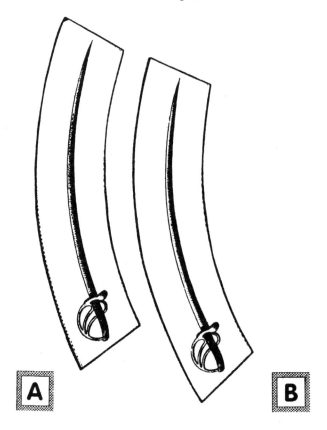

Solution: p. 254.

RUNNING OF THE BULLS

Which of these two bulls looks the larger?

Solution: p. 254.

NO TRUMP

Carefully look at this playing card. Can you figure out which distance is greater, **A-B** or **B-C**?

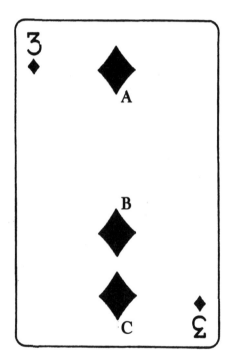

Solution: p. 254.

MORE DIAMONDS

Which is greater, the distance from **1** to **2** or **3** to **4**?

Solution: p. 254.

SWING TIME

Look at the girl on this swing. Which looks longer, the upright or the horizontal bar?

Solution: p. 254.

WHAT KEY?

These two keys have been drawn in a parallelogram. Is one bigger than the other?

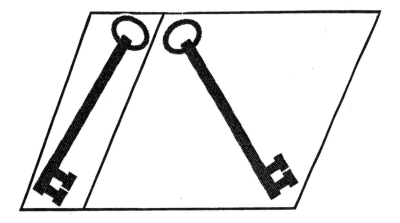

Solution: p. 254.

PICKUP STICKS

Does Line **B** look
longer or shorter than
Lines **A** and **C** ?

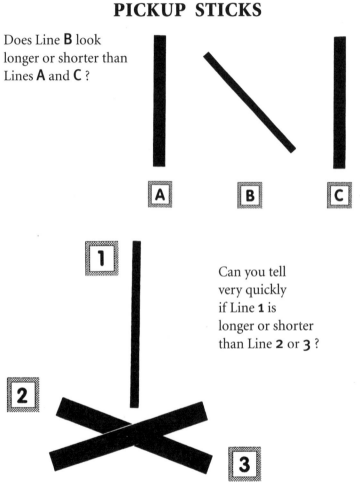

Can you tell
very quickly
if Line **1** is
longer or shorter
than Line **2** or **3** ?

Solutions: 255.

CHOPSTICKS

Using just your eyes, can you decide which is the longest line?

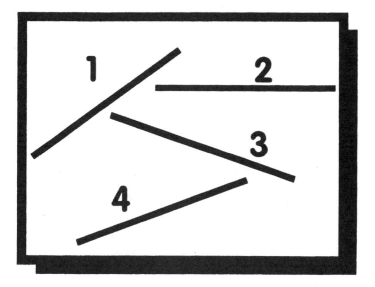

Solution: p. 255.

MR. HORACE GOLDIN

Magician Horace Goldin used this flyer to publicize his theater shows. Who looks taller, Goldin as a man or as a boy?

Solution: p. 255.

ON THE RIGHT TRACK

Which of the two rectangles looks longer, **A** or **B**?

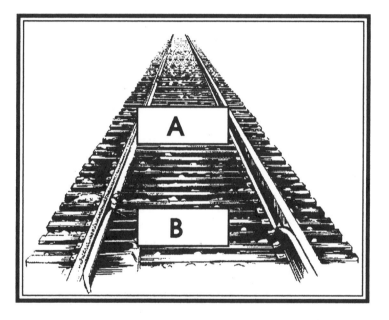

Solution: p. 255.

THAT'S IMPOSSIBLE!

IMPOSSIBLE!

Look at the object below. Whichever way you look at it, this is an "impossible" object. That is, it is possible to draw it on paper, but you could never build it out of cardboard or wood.

If it looks perfectly all right to you, look again—starting at the base of the object and then letting your eye move up.

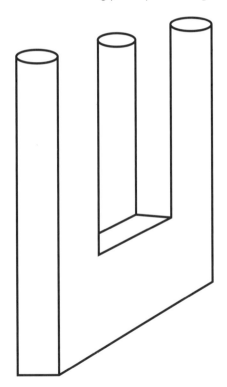

THE ETERNAL STAIRCASE

Can you figure out which corner of the staircase is the highest? Probably not. Because this is not a real staircase—it's an "impossible figure." The drawing works because your brain recognizes it as three-dimensional, and a good deal of it is realistic. The first time you glance at it, the steps look quite logical. It is only when you study the drawing closely that you see the entire structure is impossible.

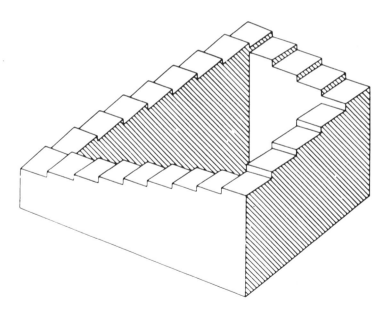

INFINITY TRIANGLE

Even if you were an expert carpenter, you would never be able to construct this figure. Each of the three joints in the triangle is drawn with great accuracy, but the rods connecting them are not!

The fascinating thing about these illusions is that your brain is so convinced they are drawings of three-dimensional figures. It takes work to see them as the flat outline drawings they are.

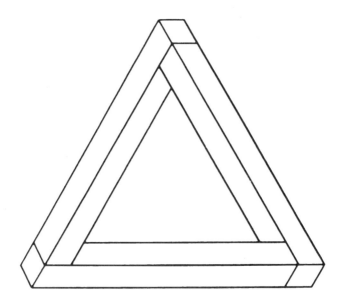

WOODSHOP DILEMMA

A practical-looking construction, but could you build it?

Solution: p. 255.

MASTER CARPENTER

Ask some friends if they can build this hollow crate for you from 12 pieces of wood. Tell them they can have $1,000 if they succeed!

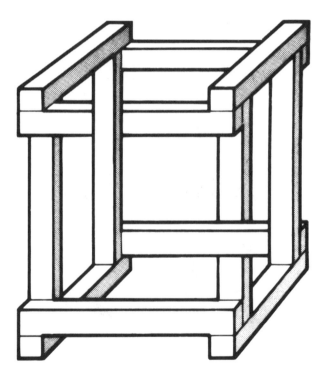

Solution: p. 255.

PENCIL PUZZLER

Can you use these disappearing pencils for writing secret messages?

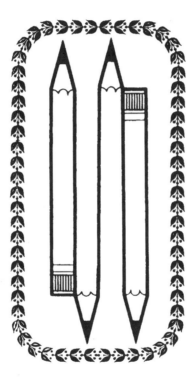

Solution: p. 255.

PITCH IN

How many prongs are there on this fork? Do you see two or three?

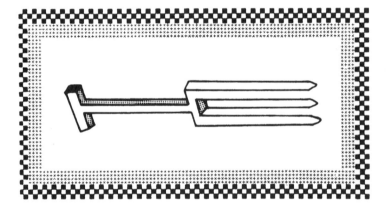

Solution: p. 255.

STACK 'EM TO THE STARS

What's the matter with these cubes?

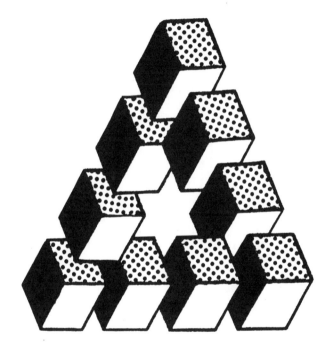

Solution: p. 255.

MAGIC MENORAH

How many candles are there?

Solution: p. 256.

CRAZY CANDELABRUM

What's wrong with this picture?

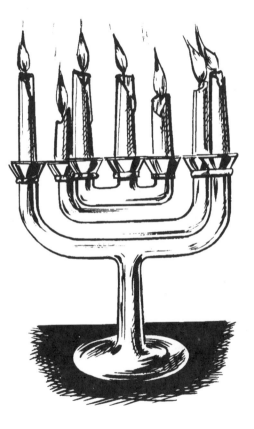

Solution: p. 256.

BROTHERS BILLY AND BOBBY

Study this picture. Do you notice anything unusual?

Solution: p. 256.

BEST FOOT FORWARD

This elephant is weird. What is his problem?

Solution: p. 256.

BEDAZZLING

COSMIC FLOWER

Take a look at the way the design at left pulsates. When you look at anything that is close to you, the muscles around your eyes pull into a spherical shape to get the words and pictures in focus. Because the lens of your eye isn't perfectly round, however, some parts of what you are looking at will be in focus, and others will look blurry. Normally, the differences in the clarity of your vision are on the outer edge of the object you are seeing, so you can still read the words and recognize the pictures. But in an illusion, such as this one—where all the lines come from different angles and meet at the center—it is impossible for you to focus clearly on all of it at once.

Your eyes are always making tiny movements that you cannot prevent, no matter how hard you try. So the clear parts of the design and the blurry parts are constantly changing. This is called "optical distortion," and it is what makes the picture seem to move, shimmer, swirl, or pulsate!

RADIANT ROSE

Stare at this figure for a time. What appears to happen?

Solution: p. 256.

CHRYSANTHEMUM

When you look at this design, you get the impression that it is not flat, but three-dimensional. Some parts of the illusion appear higher, and some lower—giving the impression of depth.

However, if you look at the curved lines that define the bumps and hollows of the flower, you will see something curious. Follow the curve that defines the outer edge of the flower right around the circle. In some places the curved lines seem to define a hump, and at others a hollow.

This object could not exist in three dimensions. Along with being another shimmering example of optical distortion, "Chrysanthemum" is an example of an impossible figure.

MAKING WAVES

Stare at this optical illusion for a while, and the curved lines seem to form the crests and valleys of waves. They may even seem to move. If you stare some more, you may also see phantom lines of color—especially in bright light, where the curved lines run parallel to each other—between the valleys and crests of the waves.

In this illusion, the restless "motion" of the waves is caused by optical distortion.

SHIMMERING SQUARES

In the effect you see at left, the shimmering is more optical distortion. This illusion is unusual because all the lines in it are sloped either forward at 45° or backward at 135°. To see why this helps make the illusion more interesting, try the following experiment.

Concentrate hard on one of the rows of lines that are sloped at 45°— like the bottom edge of a square. You'll find that all the squares formed by lines sloped at 45° appear steady, while the ones formed by lines sloping backwards at 135° look blurry and faint and seem to shimmer.

Then concentrate on a row of lines sloped at 135°. And you'll see that all the squares formed with lines sloped at 45° will look blurry and faint and seem to shimmer.

This effect occurs because your eyes cannot focus on all of the illusion at once. The parts of the illusion that you do focus on will appear clear, while the parts of the illusion that are out of focus will look blurry.

ALL SQUARE

This optical illusion is especially puzzling. If you study it closely, the ovals in the middle first seem to bulge out, and then they seem to recede.

When your eyes scan the design from left to right, the position of the ovals suggests to your brain that the ovals are popping out. But then your eyes go back over the picture. With so many different ways to scan the illusion, and no clues as to which way is "right"—you may see the ovals recede, or do any number of interesting tricks.

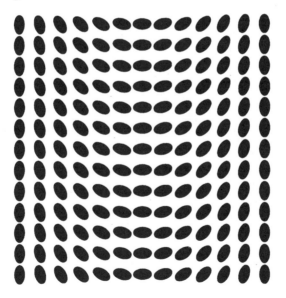

TRICKY TILES

What makes this design vibrate? Yes—optical distortion again!
The repetition of the same design on each tile helps to make this
illusion even more effective.

EYE DAZZLER

Look at this page for long enough, and your mind will really begin to boggle.

What can you see? Rows of triangles? Rows of squares? Rows of open boxes seen from above? Or a mixture of different patterns that keep changing as you look at them?

Solution: p. 256.

JESTER

If you look at this circular checkerboard closely, it will seem to pulsate and shimmer. You may also see the black-and-white patches link up to form the petals of a flower.

The shimmering that you see is caused by optical distortion, but the petals formed by your brain are an example of another phenomenon called "good continuation." It happens because your brain is trying to make sense out of what it sees. It seeks out shapes or patterns that it recognizes. Sometimes it works so hard and so cleverly that it imagines an object that isn't really there. And then we have an optical illusion.

FAIR 'N' SQUARE?

Look at the pattern in the top square. The square below is exactly the same design, but some of the squares have been filled in. How has this altered the appearance of the design?

Solution: p. 256.

CRISSCROSS

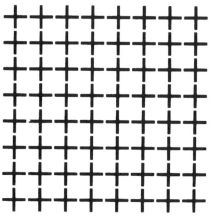

In this neat illusion, tiny white dots appear to join together to form phantom white crosses. This is another example of good continuation—your brain trying to make sense of the visual information it is receiving.

Another fascinating phenomenon—you can see tiny grey dots in the center of the black crosses. Why? Special cells in your visual system respond strongly to small patches of light and dark. If a small light patch is surrounded by more light, these cells will not respond so strongly to the small patch of light in the middle. If a small dark patch is surrounded by more darkness, these cells will not respond so strongly to the small patch of dark in the middle. So, in the case of the black crosses, your visual system does not respond fully to the centers, and you see them as grey instead.

You *can* force your eyes and brain not to "overlook" the midpoint of the crosses, if you focus your eyes and attention on one cross at a time.

STAR SPANGLED

Keep staring at this design under a bright light. After a while, what do you see?

Solution: p. 256.

ZINNIA

When you look at this illusion, you may see some grey or white spots at the points where the black lines meet. This is caused by your eyes' response to dark and light, as in "Crisscross."

HONEYCOMB

Look at this pattern long enough, and you'll find the circles begin to look like hexagons!

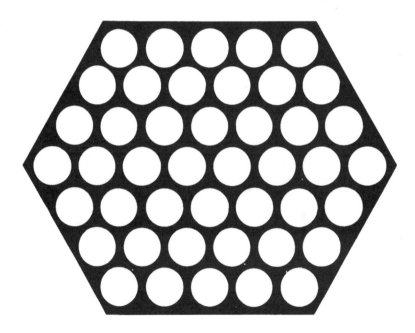

LATTICE

Here is an example of the role that contrast plays in your perceptions. Although there are only two colors, black and white, used in this design, the tiny white dots, where the black lines intersect, seem brighter and whiter than the larger white squares. This is because the tiny white squares are more completely surrounded by the black lines than the larger white squares.

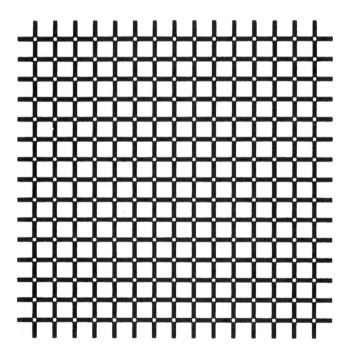

GRID

What shows up on the intersecting white lines, even though they are all white? Now, concentrate very hard on a point in the white field of intersecting lines for about 30 seconds, then quickly shift your attention to one of the black squares. What do you see inside the black squares?

Solution: p. 257.

SHADES OF GREY

Look at the grids on these two pages.

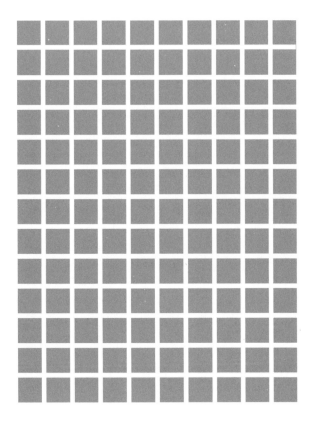

Which grey area is brighter?

Solution: p. 257.

SQUARE'S SQUARE

This illusion may remind you of "Shimmering Squares," in which lines drawn at different angles confuse the brain. Here the squares drawn on the background pattern may look bent, but in actual fact they are perfectly straight!

This is an example of the "Zollner effect," where straight lines appear to bend if they intersect with, or are seen against a background of, curved lines or lines drawn at different angles. Your eyes and brain are trying to make the straight lines fit into the background pattern.

SPIRAL SQUARE-CASE

The squares in the foreground look as if they are bent, right? This is another example of the Zollner effect. If you hold a ruler alongside them, you willl see that the lines in the square are truly straight, but the curves of the spiral background make the square seem bent.

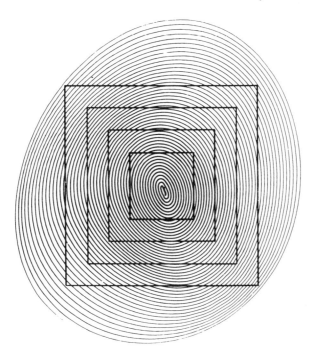

STRAIGHT AND NARROW

1) Do the horizontal lines **A** dip in the center and the lines **B** bulge in the center?

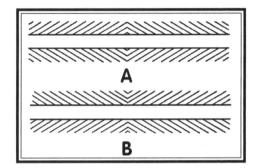

2) Are the letters of this word straight?

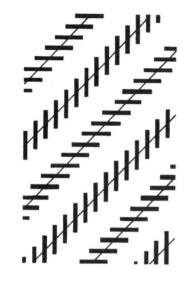

3) Are the thin lines parallel to each other?

Or crooked?

4) Are these bricks in straight rows, or have they been built in a haphazard way?

Solutions: p. 257.

DOWN THE DRAIN

Are these real circles?

Is this a spiral?

Solutions: p. 257.

SEASICK CIRCLES

If you watch this drawing while you turn the book around in a circle, you will be able to see a series of spirals moving up and down in three dimensions.

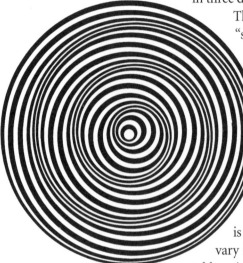

This is what's called a "stereokinetic effect." It's the result of a complex series of interactions between your eyes and your brain.

When this design is rotated, the images sent to your brain are constantly changing.

Because each circle is drawn with lines that vary in thickness, there is no stable point in the illusion for you to focus on. This is confusing to your brain, which likes to make orderly patterns out of what it sees. So your brain looks for another pattern and sees that some of the curved lines seem to link up to form a spiral. As the curves that form the spiral rotate and change position, each of your eyes simultaneously sends your brain a slightly different image. When your brain puts this all together, it decides that it must be seeing a spiral moving up and down.

WHEELIES

What happens when you rotate this page in a circular motion?

Solution: p. 257.

FAN-TASTIC

Rotate the page in a circular motion. What happens?

Solution: p. 257.

BULL'S-EYE

Revolve these pages, and the spirals will seem to get bigger or smaller, depending upon in which direction you are turning the book.

THE ESCALATOR

When you look closely at this illusion, you may get the impression that the horizontal panels are moving—with a tiny jerking motion—and the central panel may seem to be unexpectedly bright.

The reason that the "Escalator" seems to move is that you can't keep your eyes perfectly still, no matter how hard you try, and as your eyes move about, so does the image in the illusion.

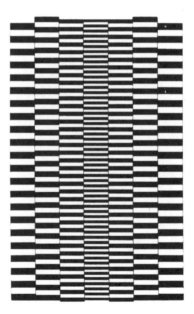

MOIRÉ GRATING

This is one of the simplest types of moiré pattern, one formed by two identical gratings. The pattern you see is so strong that it is very difficult to see the path of each individual straight line. Try tracing the path of any straight black line with your finger and you'll see.

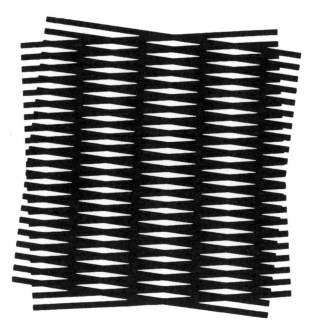

SLEIGHT OF EYE

INTRO

Seeing isn't everything. After the light impressions are gathered and sent to the brain, our minds try to put them together into something understandable. We want it to make sense, to be familiar, to be safe, so we can go on about our business.

We do this automatically—even if parts of a picture are not connected, even if parts of it are missing!—until we perceive a harmonious, satisfying "whole" that makes sense to us.

Once we find a familiar pattern, it's difficult to break up the idea, to separate its parts. The new form can become an optical illusion—such as those shown on the next few pages. We can't concentrate on just part of it because our imaginations keep putting back what we try to block out of our minds!

SPARE CHANGE

Take a look at these circles:

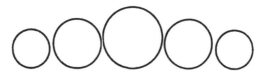

Do they sit on level ground, or do they arch upward?

Solution: p. 258.

LOOKS FAMILIAR

Without blinking, stare at this portrait under a bright light for about 30 seconds. Now gaze at a piece of white paper or a blank wall. Who do you see?

Solution: p. 258.

IN BLACK AND WHITE

Can you spot the dog? What is he an example of?

Solution: p. 258.

IT'S A SIGN

We read this sign as THE CAT, but the middle letters of each word are identical. Yet we see them as H in THE and A in CAT. Why is this?

Solution: p. 258.

SILENT MOVIES

Stare at this illustration without blinking for about 30 seconds. Now stare at a sheet of white paper or a blank wall. Who do you see?

Solution: p. 258.

SILENT SCREAM

What do these shapes represent?

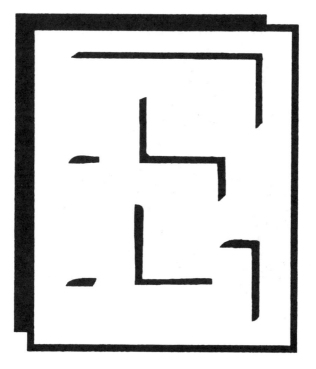

Solution: p. 258.

SADDLE UP

Part of the shoe seems to be missing. What does our brain do?

Solution: p. 258.

ARABIC?

Can you work out what these shapes represent?

Solution: p. 258.

ROHRSCHACH

This is a series of blobs and blotches, yet our brains fill in the missing bits. What do we interpret them as?

Solution: p. 258.

IN THE MIND'S EYE

These black and white dots are an illusion found in newspapers every day. When seen close up, they are meaningless. What do you see when you view them from a distance?

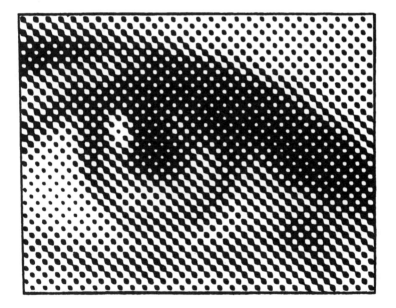

Solution: p. 258.

ABSTRACT EXPRESSIONISM

What can you uncover that is hidden in this pattern of black and white shapes?

Solution: p. 258.

Study this snow scene. You will see an animal. What is it?

Solution: p. 258.

GOT ALL YOUR MARBLES?

Can you decipher the meaning of these dots?

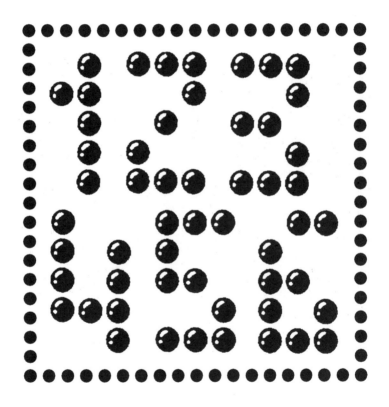

Solution: p. 259.

D-LIVER D-LETTER

The illustration below is a copy of an envelope posted in London in 1895. Hold the card as shown. Can you find out who the letter was addressed to? (This sometimes works best with one eye closed.)

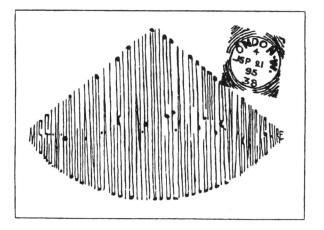

Solution: p. 259.

HIEROGLYPHICS

Can you work out what these shapes represent?

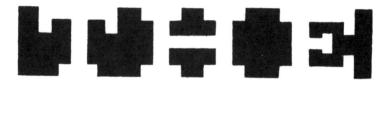

Solution: p. 259.

ENSNARED

Hold the page as in the sketch and look in the direction of the arrows. Five items will be revealed, all relating to a famous French magician from times past. Can you discover them? (This sometimes works best with one eye closed.)

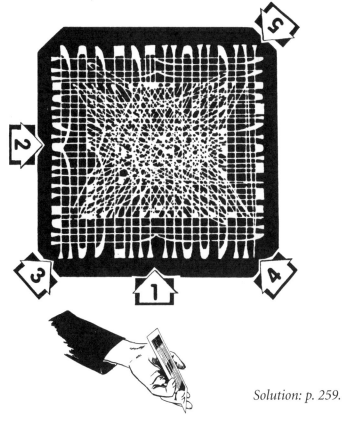

Solution: p. 259.

VERY WELL

Can you uncover the two secret messages in the circle? Hold the page as in the small sketch, and look in the direction of the arrows. This sometimes works best with one eye closed.

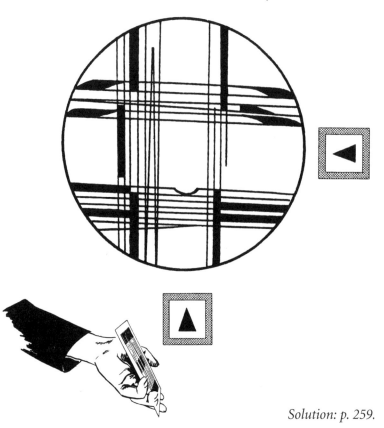

Solution: p. 259.

GOOD ADVICE

Can you discover this secret word?

Solution: p. 259.

SCREENING

This picture looks like a haphazard collection of small dashes, but if you hold the page at eye level and look in the direction of the arrow, you will uncover a word. What is it?

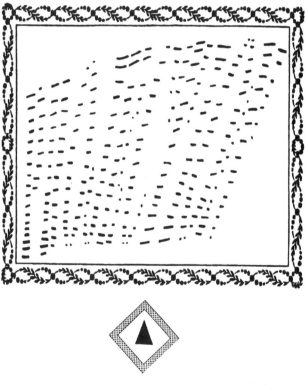

Solution: p. 259.

BRILLIANT

Stare at this bulb under a bright light for about 30 seconds. Now stare at a piece of white paper. What do you see?

Solution: p. 259.

GEOMETRICS

What do you see here, three abstract shapes or a letter of the alphabet?

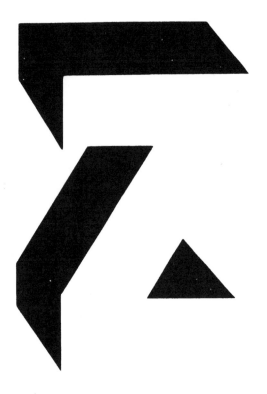

Solution: p. 259.

SIMPLY THE BEST

How can these four lines be arranged to make the number 10?

Solution: p. 259.

WHAT'S YOUR
POINT OF VIEW?

THE TEMPLE

This illusion combines two effects. It is a reversing figure: one way to look at it is as a pyramid viewed from above, with the smallest square forming the top. The other is as a passageway leading towards a tiny square door. If you look steadily at this illusion, you will probably see it flash between these two images.

It is also an example of optical distortion, because of the way it seems to shimmer.

SQUASHED CIRCLES

You can see all sorts of different effects when you look at this illusion. You may see flickering spokes radiating out from the central circle—turn the page from side to side to accentuate this effect. You can also view the central and smallest circle in two ways: as the top of a cone or as the end of a funnel.

The flickering spokes are a result of optical distortion.

PIE CUBED

Is this cube higher and wider in the back than in the front?

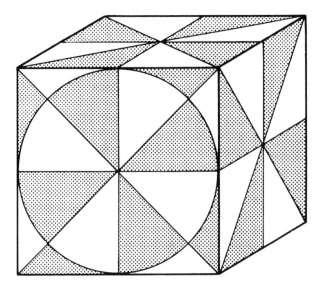

Solution: p. 260.

"E" IS FOR EYE-POPPING

Is this letter "E" toppling forward or sinking down?
Look at it steadily for half a minute.

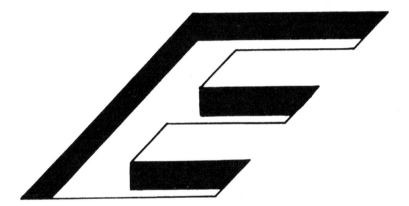

Solution: p. 260.

HEE-HAW

What is mysterious about these donkeys?

Solution: p. 260.

BANKED NOTES

Are these stacks of banknotes sloping downward to the right, or are they pointing down to the left?

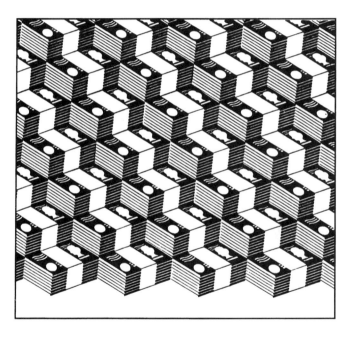

Solution: p. 260.

VINTNER'S VIEW

What do you see—black wine glasses or white vases?

Solution: p. 260.

GO FISH

What's wrong with these fish?

Solution: p. 260.

TUBULAR

Which way are the tubes facing?

Solution: p. 260.

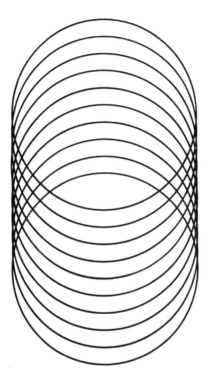

Here's an unusual tube. Look carefully at it for at least a minute, and then decide if you are looking down the tube from above it or up the tube from under it.

Solution: p. 260.

SPACE STATION

When you look at this strange construction, are you seeing it from above or below?

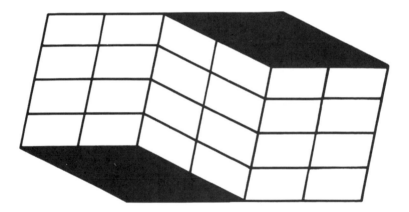

Solution: p. 260.

VIEW OF A ROOM

A very strange room. Are we inside it—or outside?

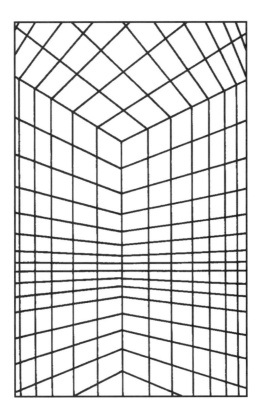

Solution: p. 260.

COUNT THE CUBES

Are there seven cubes here, or eight?

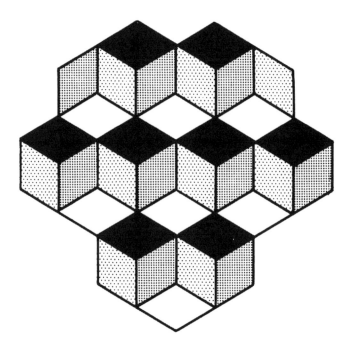

Solution: p. 261.

THE CHANGING CUBE

Is this a dark cube in a corner, or is it a white cube with a corner cut away?

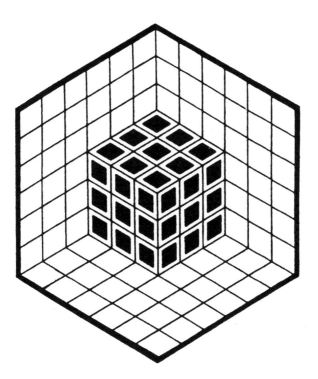

Solution: p. 261.

NEED TO KNOW

Does this sign say "Knowledge" or does it say "Ignorance"?

Solution: p. 261.

STORMY

We read this passage as "dark cloud." Is the first letter
a "c" or a "d"?

Solution: p. 261.

THE GLASS TABLE

This is a curious table. Are you looking at the table from above or below?

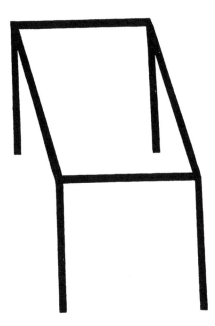

Solution: p. 261.

MEANS OF SUPPORT

Are you looking down on this cube with the diagonal line starting from the upper left-hand corner, or are you looking up at it with the diagonal line starting from the lower right-hand corner?

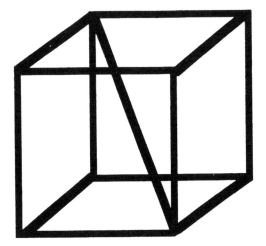

Solution: p. 261.

BAR NONE

What do you see? Most people see ten dark lines, but there is something else. What is it?

Solution: p. 261.

ON THE TILES

This item of "op art" is made up of straight lines. Stare at it for a while and what do you see?

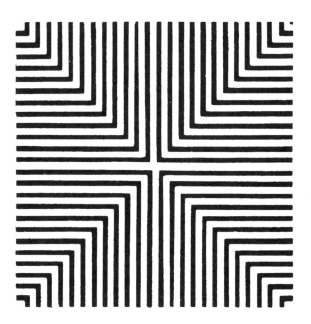

Solution: p. 261.

A-FRAME

Look at the figure on the left. Is it sloping as in Picture **1**, or does it slant as in Picture **2**?

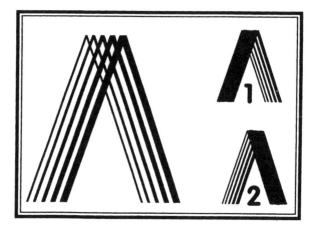

Solution: p. 261.

OUTLOOK

What do you see, the head of a Native American or an Inuit looking into a cave?

Solution: p. 261.

DOTTY

Do you see the area bounded by the darker lines as the outside of a transparent cube?

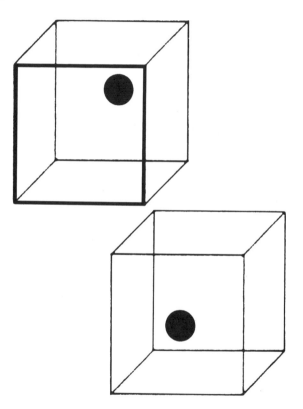

If you keep looking, the bounded area will become the inner surface of a cube tilted a different way.

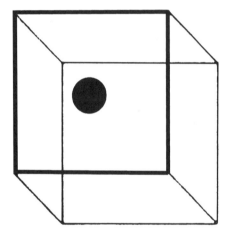

Is the black spot on the front or rear face? Or is it inside the cube?

Solution: p. 261.

POINT THE WAY

What do you see in this picture—black arrows or white arrows?

Which is it—dark arrows pointing upward or light arrows pointing downward?

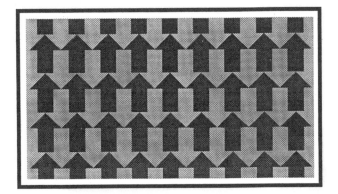

Solution: p. 261.

WHICH WAY

Which way are the letters facing? Are they pointing down to the right or up to the left?

Solution: p. 261.

Why do the fish in this illustration seem to swim in one direction and then in the other?

Solution: p. 261.

HIGH SIDE

Is the left side of this picture high, or the right side?

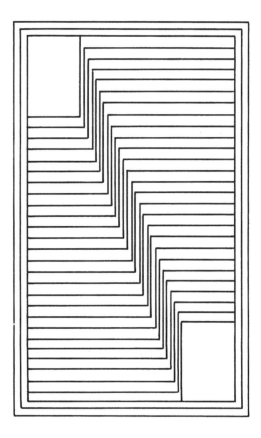

Solution: p. 262.

OP TILE

This design is made up from straight lines. Look at it for a while, and you may see other shapes. What are they?

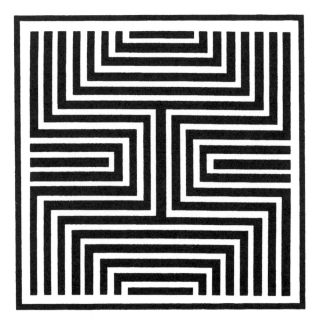

Solution: p. 262.

PIECES OF EIGHT

Which way do these bizarre numbers face, downward to the left or upward to the right?

Solution: p. 262.

THE FIRST SHALL BE LAST

It's always good to be the "first" and win, but sometimes we finish at the end of the race. What word would you use, and can you find it in this picture?

Solution: p. 262.

IN YOUR FACE

GRAM 'N' GRAMP

Which set of faces is larger?

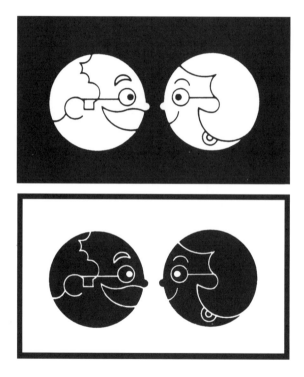

Solution: p. 262.

WATCH THE BIRDIE

Bring this page close to your face, and what happens?

Solution: p. 262.

BLOOMIN'

Which of these flowers has the larger center?

Solution: p. 262.

LITTLE GOOSE GIRL

Stare at the center of the illustration. Then slowly bring the page close to your face. What happens?

Solution: p. 262.

INTROVERT

Which circle has the greater diameter? The one below . . .

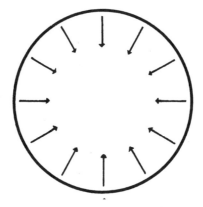

EXTROVERT

. . . or, this one?

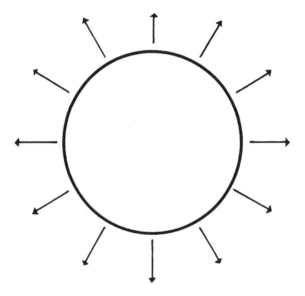

Solution: p. 262.

BESIDE HERSELF

The magician's assistant has been sawed in two halves. Can you think of a way of making her whole again?

Solution: p. 262.

ATTENTION, PLEASE!

How many times does the letter **F** appear in the paragraph below?

MAGIC HAS AN IRRESISTIBLE FASCINATION
FOR CHILDREN OF ALL AGES. THERE IS NO
FINER FORM OF ENTERTAINMENT THAN
A PERFORMANCE OF MAGIC ...
FULL OF FUN, FANTASY,
MYSTERY AND LAUGHTER.

Solution: p. 263.

NOON

There are two unusual things about this word.
Can you seen them?

Solution: p. 263.

STATUE OF LIBERTY

Read the words on the panel. What do they say? Are you sure?

Solution: p. 263.

HUNGRY SNAKE

How can you get the bird to fly into the snake's mouth?

Solution: p. 263.

CREEPY

What do the words on this haunted house mean?

Solution: p. 263.

DELUSIONS

Can you spot anything unusual in this paragraph?

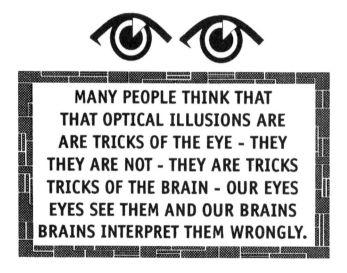

MANY PEOPLE THINK THAT
THAT OPTICAL ILLUSIONS ARE
ARE TRICKS OF THE EYE - THEY
THEY ARE NOT - THEY ARE TRICKS
TRICKS OF THE BRAIN - OUR EYES
EYES SEE THEM AND OUR BRAINS
BRAINS INTERPRET THEM WRONGLY.

Solution: p. 263.

WAKE-UP CALL

What creates the illusion of movement in this picture?

Solution: p. 263.

NETWORKING

Slowly bring this page close to your face. What happens to the butterfly?

Solution: p. 263.

FAIR AND SQUARE

Of the three squares, which one is the smallest?

Solution: p. 263.

SQUARING THE CIRCLE

Which of the two circles is the larger?

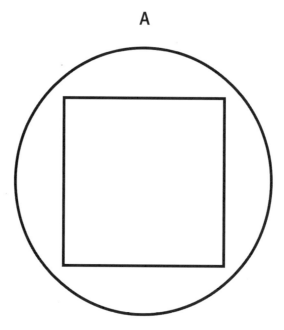

A

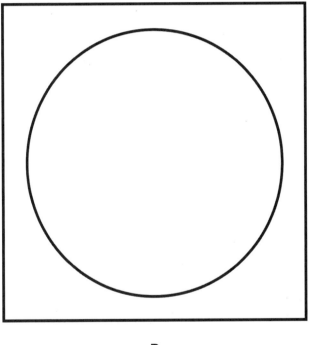

B

Solution: p. 263.

STOP OR GO?

Which of these circles are the same size, those in row **A** or
those in row **B**?

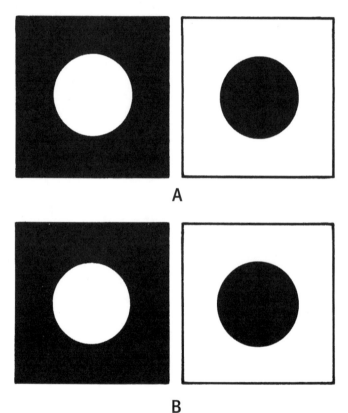

A

B

Solution: p. 263.

GO FOR THE GOAL

Are these balls the same size?

Solution: p. 264.

SEEING AURAS

Is the white circle perfect, or is it crimped at the points of the triangle?

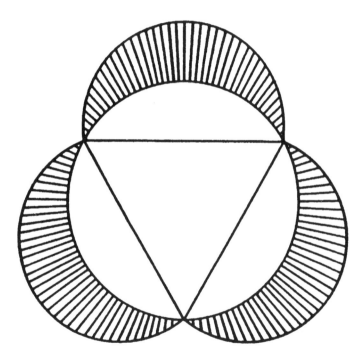

Solution: p. 264.

GET CENTERED

Which of these two dots is in the true center?

Solution: p. 264.

MON AMI PIERROT

Hold the page about three inches in front of your face, and gaze at the star and two clown hats. What happens?

Solution: p. 264.

CREEL WORLD

Hold the page at eye level, and look at the fishing rods in the direction of the arrow. What happens?

Solution: p. 264.

ASLANT

Which line connects with the letter **W**?

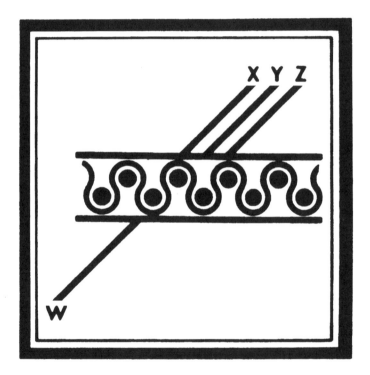

Solution: p. 264.

ASSIGNATION

Stare at the center of this illustration, and then very slowly bring the page towards your face. What happens next?

Solution: p. 264.

JOHN MARSHALL

On a very windy day this doorway created a problem for John Marshall. Can you unravel the mysterious thing that happened?

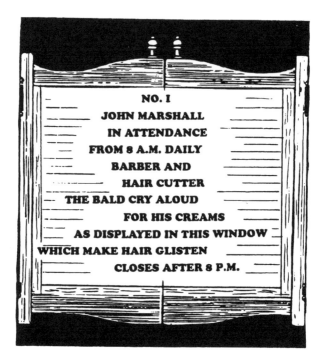

NO. I

JOHN MARSHALL

IN ATTENDANCE

FROM 8 A.M. DAILY

BARBER AND

HAIR CUTTER

THE BALD CRY ALOUD

FOR HIS CREAMS

AS DISPLAYED IN THIS WINDOW

WHICH MAKE HAIR GLISTEN

CLOSES AFTER 8 P.M.

Solution: p. 264.

YOU!

This finger is pointing straight at you. Move your head from left to right. What happens?

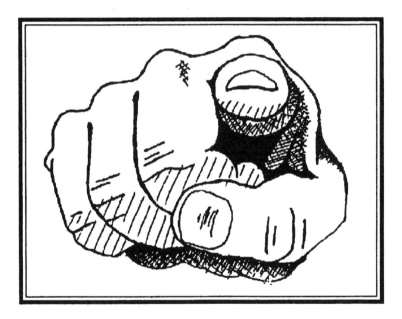

Solution: p. 264.

SEEING EYE TO EYE

Try this experiment: Sit facing a friend. Slowly move toward each other until your noses almost touch. Keep staring straight ahead. What happens to your friend's eyes? Try it to find out, or try it on yourself by looking into a mirror.

Solution: p. 264.

LOVEBIRDS

Hold this page at arm's length. Now slowly bring the page toward your face. What happens to the two birds?

Solution: p. 264.

وقمر

VISUAL

THINKING

PUZZLES

INTRO

Visual thinking uses the incredible power of your "mind's eye" to define the way we process all sorts of information. Visual thinking isn't stuck in the present. We can use it to reflect back into the past—and it can just as easily jump into the future.

The next puzzles are mind-bending challenges developed to test your visual thinking skills. Open your eyes and your mind, and have fun!

WHAT'S NEXT?

Solution: p. 265.

TABLE FOR TWO

As these two lovebirds slurp up a shared piece of spaghetti, will a knot form in the pasta?

Solution: p. 265.

GALACTICA

An astronomer photographs two side-by-side spiral galaxies. When she examines her files, however, she discovers that one of the photos is of a different galaxy pair.

Examine the six images below. One pair of spirals is unlike the others. Can you identify the different image?

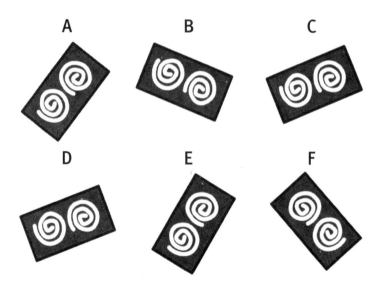

Solution: p. 265.

WHAT'S YOUR SIGN?

The mathematical signs connecting the numbers below have
been left out. Good thing we've supplied them on four tiles! Can
you place the tiles between the numbers so that the final answer
is 3? (All operations are done in left-to-right order.)

$$5 \blacksquare 2 \blacksquare 3 \blacksquare 5 \blacksquare 4 = 3$$

$$\boxed{+} \quad \boxed{-} \quad \boxed{\times} \quad \boxed{\div}$$

Solution: p. 265.

CARNY LOAD-OUT

Alas, the carnival is over, and the roustabouts are taking down the rides. The only thing left is the section of the roller-coaster track and frame shown below. To be moved, it must be divided into identical parts. Can you do it?

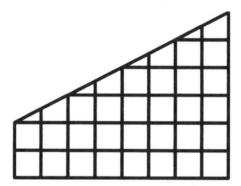

Solution: p. 265.

RACK 'EM

The billiard balls shown below are positioned in a six-ball rack. If you add the values of any three-ball edge, you will come up with ten.

Now, you've got to rearrange the billiard balls. Can you place them within this rack to produce three other patterns that also produce equal-sum sides?

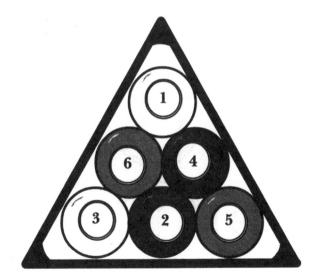

Solution: p. 266.

THE SHADOW KNOWS

Here's one more puzzle for you to visualize without an image on the page: Try to imagine a shape that can produce three different shadows.

When illuminated from below, it casts a circular shadow.

When illuminated from the north, it casts a rectangular shadow.

When illuminated from the east, it casts a triangular shadow.

What is the shape of the actual object?

STOP AND THINK

How many paths can lead you through the octagonal maze on the facing page? Before you begin, keep in mind that from start to finish, you can only move in the direction of the arrows.

There is a way to do this puzzle without tracing out each path. Can you discover the strategy?

Solution: p. 266.

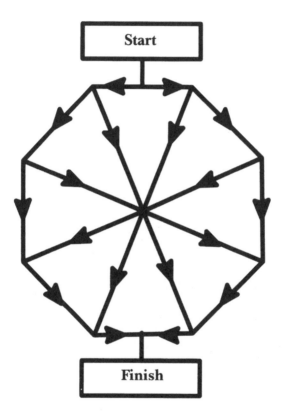

Solution: p. 267.

EQUALITY RULES

How many equilateral triangles can you see in the pattern below?

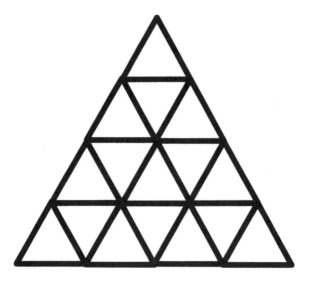

Solution: p. 267.

HIDDEN IN PLANE SITE

Can you discover fifteen squares outlined in the pattern below?

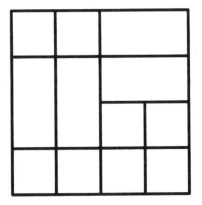

Solution: p. 267.

MORE JOE

The owners of a local cafe have ordered coffee pots in two sizes. If coffee pot **A** makes around eight cups of tasty java, about how many cups can be made in **B** ?

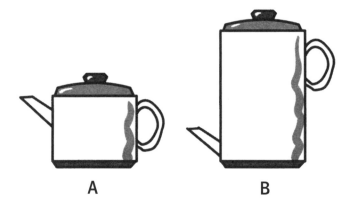

A   **B**

Solution: p. 267.

GYM RAT

Are the belts and wheels arranged to spin freely as this quizzical rodent races up the treadmill?

Solution: p. 267.

PROFILING

Even though you can't see the entire block structure below, you can make accurate statements about its appearance. If viewed from all directions, which one of the four profiles shown on the facing page is impossible?

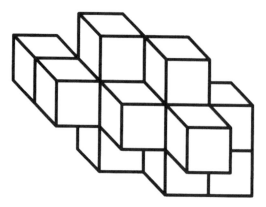

A

B

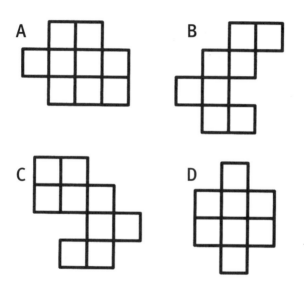

C

D

Solution: p. 268.

LINK LATCH

While digging through a box of metal links, a jeweler uncovers the three joined links shown below. She decides to separate the links and begins to examine them.

After a while, she discovers a way to disconnect all three by opening just a single link! Can you tell which one that is?

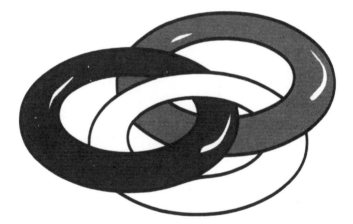

Solution: p. 268.

AMAZE-ING STRING

Shown below is an odd loop of string, with a pipe located at the center of the string.

If the string is pulled by its two free ends, will it come free of the pipe? Or will the string get caught by the pipe?

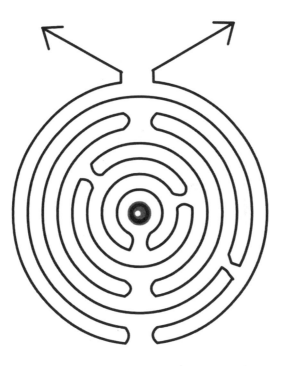

Solution: p. 268.

PENCIL STACK

Which is the third pencil up from the bottom of the stack?

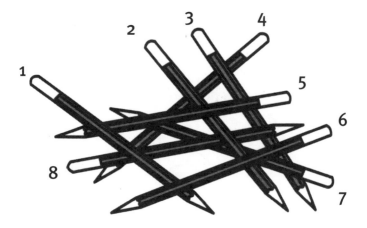

Solution: p. 268.

NAUGHTY NOTES

And now, a musical distraction . . . . Which pair of notes is unlike the other six pairs?

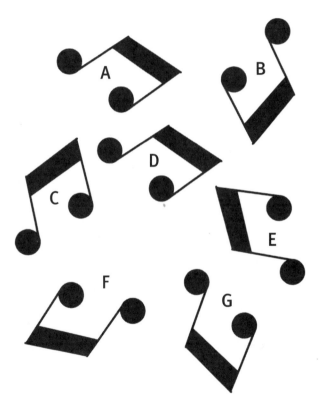

Solution: p. 268.

REFLECTING BACK

Imagine the hands of a standard clock in the position that indicates the time is 4:20. Suppose you looked at that clock in a mirror. Which of these clock faces would the reflected image resemble?

I   II   III   IV

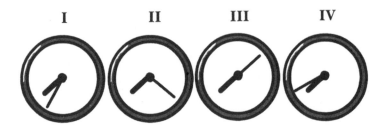

Solution: p. 269.

OK, let's make it a bit more challenging. Suppose that the hands of a clock indicate the time is 2:40. Suppose you turned the clock upside down and then looked at its mirror reflection. Which one of these faces would the reflected image resemble?

I   II   III   IV

Solution: p. 269.

MIRROR MADNESS

Do you realize that your brain is constantly trying to make sense of the information sent to it by your eyes?

As you may already know, the image that falls upon the retina of your eye is upside down. Your brain, however, flips the image over into a more logical upright appearance. Use that talent to answer this riddle: "Mirror, mirror, on the wall, which of the choices, **A** through **D**, is a reflection of the larger tile?"

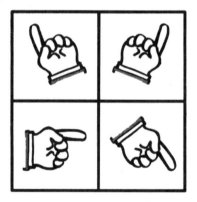

A

B

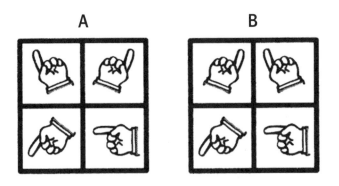

C

D

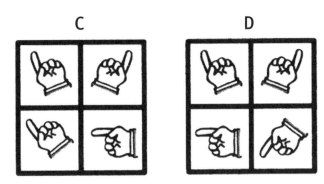

Solution: p. 269.

WRAP IT UP

You don't need a crystal ball to see into the future. All you need is your brain.

The shape below is formed from three smaller pieces. These pieces are connected by a tiny hinge at their point of attachment. Suppose you were able to rotate the pieces so the neighboring sides aligned flatly and squarely. Which one of the shapes below could this structure look alike?

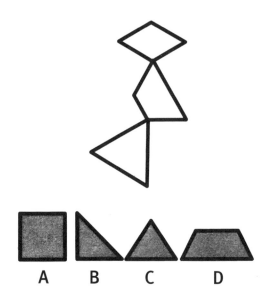

A   B   C   D

Solution: p. 269.

PHARAOH FOLDS

Which of the folding patterns below will produce a shape unlike the others?

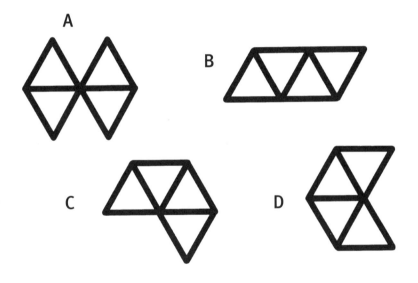

Solution: p. 270.

PI PIECES

There are many skills we associate with visual thinking. Some of these skills may be much more difficult to master than others. For example, the ability to rotate objects mentally is often harder than we might imagine.

Try this: If you were to assemble these pieces into a circle, what would the figure formed by the inner lines look like?

Solution: p. 270.

BLOCK HEADS

Which pattern of blocks is unlike the others?

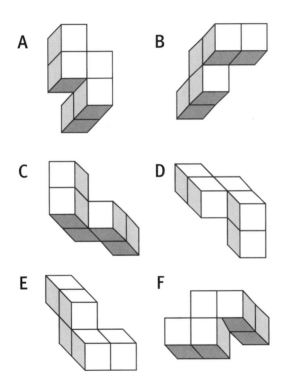

A

B

C

D

E

F

Solution: p. 270.

ON THE MARCH

An army of neurotic ants lives in the jungle of some remote country. In their journey they've uncovered a trail formed by three overlapping circles.

Here's the challenge: The ants have to find a route that covers every part of this odd trail. The route can't cross over itself (nor can the ants back up and retrace any steps). Can you uncover their continuous route?

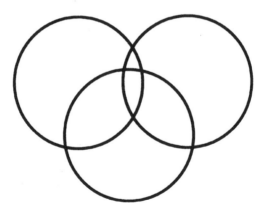

Solution: p. 270.

Another route with the same restrictions.

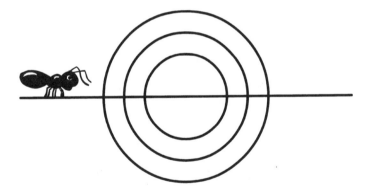

Solution: p. 270.

ROLL WITH IT

If you rolled this pattern into a cylinder, which one of the choices below will it look like?

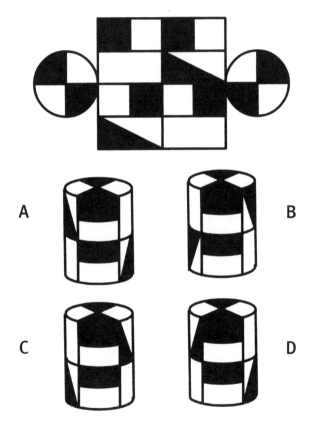

Solution: p. 270.

FROM WHENCE IT CAME?

Now let's reverse the thinking process. Can you identify the outer pattern from which the cube was folded?

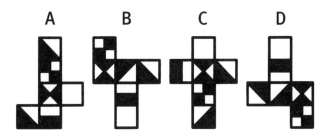

A   B   C   D

Solution: p. 270.

HIDDEN PICTURES
HIDDEN FIGURES

INTRO

The geometric puzzles you will find in this section show how difficult it can be to see familiar shapes and figures when they are in unfamiliar surroundings. Each shape is hidden once, in the same size, inside its corresponding drawing. Can you find the shapes with your naked eye, or must you resort to paper and pencil?

Most of the picture puzzles here are from bygone days. The pictures may look ordinary, but they are really great examples of the art of illusion. If you didn't know there were pictures hidden inside the pictures, you might never guess at what you were missing. Look again!

TWINKLE, TWINKLE

This star is hidden among the designs in the drawing below. Where is it hiding?

Solution: p. 271.

NAPOLEON IN EXILE

Can you see where Napoleon is hiding?

Solution: p. 271.

SWEET VIOLETS

Napoleon's supporters used to wear violets as a sign of their allegiance. This print hides the faces of Napoleon, Maria Louisa, and the young King of Rome. Can you find them?

Solution: p. 271.

I'LL BE WAITING

The sailor is looking through the telescope to find his girlfriend. Can you find her?

Solution: p. 271.

SCHIZOID

This old design is called three faces under one hat. Can you guess why?

Solution: p. 271.

OPTICAL OCTAGON

Can you locate the octagon in the design?

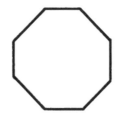

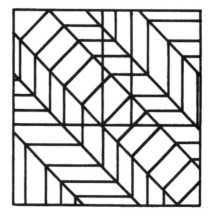

Solution: p. 271.

CROSSED

Where is the cross in the square?

Solution: p. 272.

CHIN CHIN!

This picture is based on a Victorian "Fantasy Face"—love of the clown. What do you see in this print?

Solution: p. 272.

VERBEEK

Look carefully at this picture by the great Dutch artist Verbeek—then turn it upside down, and give yourself a surprise.

JUST AS HE REACHES A SMALL,
GRASSY POINT OF LAND, A LARGE FISH ATTACKS HIM,
LASHING FURIOUSLY WITH HIS TAIL.

LOVING CUP

What do you see? Two people looking at each other or a fancy vase?

Solution: p. 272.

CHECK . . . MATE

Study this chess piece very carefully. What else can you see?

Solution: p. 272.

DOBBIN

Dobbin the horse has an animal bodyguard. Which animal is it?

Solution: p. 272.

M' LORD

This old-time print shows a boy and his father.
Can you find both of them?

Solution: p. 272.

DAISY

Daisy the Cow is rather timid. She is even afraid of a frog. Can you think of a way of transforming her into one?

Solution: p. 272.

M' LADY

This Victorian print shows an old lady and a young woman.
Can you find both of them?

Solution: p. 272.

FIND THE MISSING BOATS

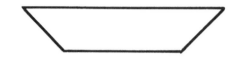

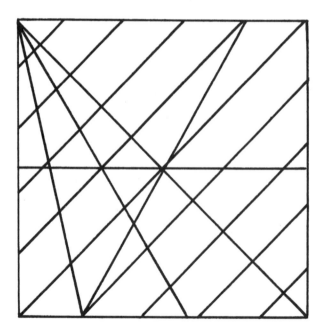

Solution: p. 273.

Solution: p. 273.

TUMBLING CHERUBS

How many children can you see in this vintage etching?

Solution: p. 273.

VANITY

What do you see in this Edwardian print?

Solution: p. 273.

SEEING SANTA

This quaint Christmas scene conceals the face of Santa Claus. Where is he hiding?

Solution: p. 273.

UNDER THE MISTLETOE

What's odd about the drawing?

Solution: p. 273.

KINGDOM COW

Observe this cow very carefully.
Do you notice anything unusual about it?

Solution: p. 273.

TIGER, TIGER

This is a sketch from World War I.
Can you find the kaiser hiding in this tiger design?

Solution: p. 273.

HIDDEN HOUSE

Can you locate the house shape in the grid below?

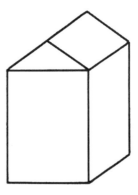

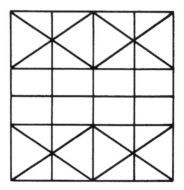

Solution: p. 274.

OCTA-GONE?

Can your eye find the octagon in the squares shown below?

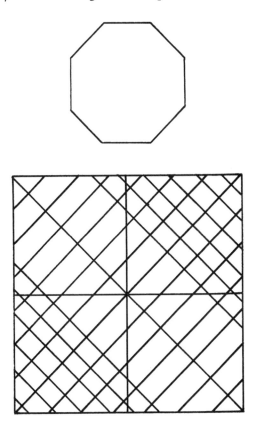

Solution: p. 274.

OLD MOTHER HUBBARD

Old Mother Hubbard is resting comfortably in her shoe. Where is her landlord?

Her dog has startled poor Mother Hubbard. Where is her butler?

Solution: p. 275.

Mother Hubbard is serving tea to her children, but five of them are missing. Can you find them?

Solution: p. 275.

THERE BE GIANTS

In this woodland scene two giants are searching for a girl. Can you find all three in this picture?

Solution: p. 276.

FOOLISH LOVE

Look at this print close up, and you will see it is two people saying farewell. Now view the page from a distance. What do you see?

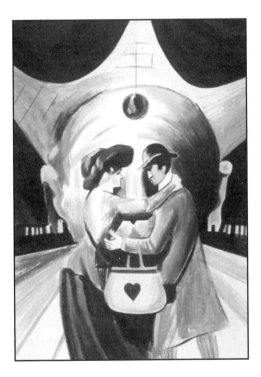

Solution: p. 276.

STRUTTING HIS STUFF

The proud peacock has a proud owner. Can you see where he is?

Solution: p. 276.

OLD STONE-FACE

This is a magnificent landscape. Can you find the landlord?

Solution: p. 276.

SPY SEARCH

The soldiers are looking for the spy, but they can't find him.
Can you?

Solution: p. 276.

GOSSIP

This print is an a Edwardian design entitled "Gossip," in which two ladies are in discussion. Look at the page from a distance, and what do you see?

Solution: p. 276.

PACHYDERM

This elephant is unique. Can you figure out why?

Solution: p. 276.

SOLUTIONS

THE LONG AND
THE SHORT OF IT

Blockbuster (page 2)—No. Both blocks are the same size. If they look unequal in size, it's because of the different black lengths on either side of them.

Right Angle? (page 3)—The angles are the same! They *look* unequal because of the other angles on either side of them, which *are* different.

A Question of Lines (page 4)—All three are the same length. It is the *angles* that make the horizontal lines look like different lengths.

A Question of Angles (page 5)—Both lines are the same length. Once again, it is the angles the lines make that cause them to look unequal.

How Far This Time? (page 6)—It looks greater, but in fact it's the same.

Point of View (page 7)—Both are exactly the same length. It's the difference in position that makes the lower one *look* longer.

A Curve Ball (page 8)—All three are arcs from *the same circle*, but the more you see of each arc, the greater the curve seems to be.

From Here to There (page 9)—It *looks* longer, but both lines are actually the same length.

Parallel Bars (page 10)—**A-B** *looks* a lot longer, but both lines are the same length. Check with a ruler if you don't believe it.

Thick and Thin (page 11)—The two thin lines are of equal lengths.

Fiddlesticks (page 12)—Both horizontal lines are the same length. It's the converging lines that make the top line look longer.

Popcorn, Anyone? (page 13)—They are all the same height. The man at the right looks tallest. We expect things to look smaller when they are farther away. The man at the right is farthest away, and we would expect him to look the smallest. Since he doesn't, we assume he's really larger than the others.

Investigate This (page 14)—The four detectives have equally large mouths.

Clips and Pins (page 15)—They are both the same height and width. The one with the horizontal stripes looks wider because your eyes follow the horizontal lines.

Blinded by the Light (page 16–17)—They are both the same height and width. The one with the horizontal stripes looks wider because your eyes follow the horizontal lines.

Sawtooth (page 18)—Height and width are the same.

Make Your Point (page 19)—It is exactly in the center.

Paper Airplanes (page 20–21)—The crossbars are exactly in the center of the triangles. (page 21)—No, they are both the same size. This is another example of the difficulty of judging size when angles are involved.

Dumbbells (page 22)—Line **A** equals **B** and **C** equals **D**. Line **A** seems longer than **B** because we unconsciously add the circles on the end of the line to its length. The same is true of line **C** with its open square. In each figure, **A** equals **B**.

High Hat (page 23)—They are the same.

Bell Tower (page 24)—The height of the tower is the same as the width of the church (including the base of the tower).

Passing Lanes (page 25)—Left: Yes, but when you break a straight line with a solid bar, the straight line seems displaced. Right: **B** is the continuation of **A**. **C** looks as though it connects with **A** because the solid bar "displaces" the line.

Centerfolds (page 26–27)—The center lines in drawings **A** through **F** are all the same height. The only differences are the angles of the lines leading away from them.

In the Arena (page 28)—The sections are all the same size—one-quarter of the whole circle.

Florence Nightingale (page 29)—They are both the same size. Trace one of them, and measure it against the other.

Fishtale (page 30)—After you make a guess, use a ruler to check. In this illusion, the outside lines help to convince us that the bottom fish is bigger.

Chameleons (page 31)—They are the same size, but the arrows make us think that the lower lizard is bigger than its friend.

High Dive (page 32)—The blocks are exactly the same size, though the white one looks bigger. This is another illusion in which the background design confuses us.

Zip Your Lip (page 33)—Both mouths are identical. The arrows at the end of the lines confuse us.

Coup de Grâce (page 34)—They are both the same size. It's the curve that confuses us.

Running of the Bulls (page 35)—Both bulls are identical in size.

No Trump (page 36)—Both distances are identical.

More Diamonds (page 37)—They are both the same distance.

Swing Time (page 38)—Both lines are the same length. The upright line appears to look longer.

What Key? (page 39)—Both keys are identical in size.

Pickup Sticks (page 40)—Both lines are the same length. All three lines are the same length.

Chopsticks (page 41)—Line 3 is the longest.

Mr. Horace Goldin (page 42)—They are both the same height.

On the Right Track (page 43)—They are both the same size, although **A** should appear longer.

THAT'S IMPOSSIBLE!

Woodshop Dilemma (page 49)—Never. This is a trick drawing—another impossible object!

Master Carpenter (page 50)—Don't worry, your money's safe. No matter how skilled your friends may be in carpentry, they will never be able to build this crate. It's an impossible object.

Pencil Puzzler (page 51)—These are impossible pencils so that while you can draw them, you can't use them!

Pitch In (page 52)—It's an impossible fork! You couldn't make one, but maybe you can draw it...

Stack 'em to the Stars (page 53)—They form an impossible triangle! The idea was first drawn in Sweden in 1934 by Oscar Reutersvard.

Magic Menorah (page 54)—First count the flames—five. Now count the base of each candle, and you'll find there are seven.

Crazy Candelabrum (page 55)—A number of the holders seem to be suspended in midair!

Brothers Billy and Bobby (page 56)—The boys are sitting on an impossible staircase. Study the picture. The top stair becomes the middle stair, and vice versa.

Best Foot Forward (page 57)—It's an impossible elephant. Look at its legs — can you figure them out?

BEDAZZLING

Radiant Rose (page 61)—The rays will appear to pulse and vibrate.

Eye Dazzler (page 67)—All of these effects can be seen in this image.

Fair 'n' Square? (page 69)—It takes on a curved appearance.

Star Spangled (page 71)—You see flashing white stars bouncing among the black stars. Try to focus on these "afterimages" and they will vanish.

Grid (page 75)—You see an even blacker lattice design inside the black squares! This is the result of your eyes being tired of seeing the white lines—so they record the black instead when you look away.

Shades of Grey (page 76–77)—Both grey areas have the same intensity. The white lines, though, make the area on the left seem brighter.

Straight and Narrow (page 80–81)—1) It's just an illusion. Both sets of lines are parallel. 2) The letters are perfectly upright. The background pattern confuses us. 3) Exactly parallel. The thicker crosshatch lines just give the illusion that they are bending. Some scientists say this is because we can't judge the size of angles well. Others say the cross-lines distract us. 4) They are in straight rows. Place a ruler on them to check.

Down the Drain (page 82–83)—Yes. To prove it, trace round one of them with a compass. (page 83)—No, it's a series of circles within circles. Check it by tracing them with your finger. This illusion is known as the Fraser Spiral.

Wheelies (page 85)—Each circle will seem to revolve on its axis. The inner cog wheel will appear to rotate in the opposite direction.

Fan-tastic (page 86)—A small grey disk appears in the center of the spokes.

SLEIGHT OF EYE

Spare Change (page 92)—They all sit on level ground.

Looks Familiar (page 93)—Abraham Lincoln.

In Black and White (page 94)—This is an example of "closure." Your brain fills in the missing bits.

It's A Sign (page 95)—Our brain is trying to make sense of what we see, so it leaps ahead, closes up the top of the second **H**, and reads it as an **A**.

Silent Movies (page 96)—Charlie Chaplin.

Silent Scream (page 97)—A letter "E."

Saddle Up (page 98)—Our brain fills in the missing bits, and we perceive it as a pair of shoes. This is an example of a "closure."

Arabic? (page 99)—The number 6.

Rohrschach (page 100)—The head of a man with curly hair and a mustache.

In the Mind's Eye (page 101)—An eye.

Abstract Expressionism (page 102)—A bearded man's head. See illustration at the right. (page 103)—A dalmation dog.

Got All Your Marbles? (page 104)—The numbers 1, 2, 3, 4, 5, 6. Viewing the page from a distance helps.

D-Liver D-Letter (page 105)—Miss S.I.M. Holland, Albion House, Alcester, Warwickshire.

Hieroglyphics (page 106)—It's the words "THE" and "Eye." Focus your attention on the white areas of the shapes.

Ensnared (page 107)—All the words are about the French magician Jean-Eugène Robert-Houdin, who was born in 1805 and is regarded as the father of modern-day magic: 1. Robert-Houdin, 2. Prestidigitateur (French for "magician"), 3. St. Blois (place near where he was born), 4. Physicien, 5. Mecanicien.

Very Well (page 108)—The messages are: 1. How is. 2. your Dad.

Good Advice (page 109)—The secret word is "LAUGH." Look at the page at eye level in the direction of the arrow.

Screening (page 110)—The word "Projection."

Brilliant (page 111)—You will see a lighted bulb.

Geometrics (page 112)—It's the letter "Z."

Simply the Best (page 113)—Cover up the top and bottom of the illustration with your hands, and you will see the number 10.

WHAT'S YOUR POINT OF VIEW?

Pie Cubed (page 118)—No, but it seems higher and wider in the back because of the way it has been drawn. We expect the back of it to be further away and to look smaller. Since it is the same size, we automatically assume it is bigger in the back.

"E" Is for Eye-Popping (page 119)—Both are possible. It depends on how you look at it.

Hee-Haw (page 120)—The three donkeys have only three ears between them!

Banked Notes (page 121)—Either one. The design reverses.

Vintner's View (page 122)—Take your pick!

Go Fish (page 123)—Between them, these strange fish have only one head.

Tubular (page 124)—Each tube can be seen to open in different directions. (page 125)—You can look at the tube either way. Sometimes you'll feel you're seeing through it from the top, and sometimes from the bottom!

Space Station (page 126)—This is one of those odd figures that you feel you are seeing from above at one moment and from below at the next. Whichever way you look at it, it's still confusing!

View of a Room (page 127)—Either one.

Count the Cubes (page 128)—Both. There are eight cubes with black tops, or seven cubes with white bottoms!

The Changing Cube (page 129)—Either answer is correct.

Need to Know (page 130)—The choice is yours.

Stormy (page 131)—It's both. It depends on what you read first—the horizontal or vertical word.

The Glass Table (page 132)—The table can be seen in both views. It flip-flops.

Means of Support (page 133)—You can see this any way you want.

Bar None (pg. 134)—A star is formed in the center of the design.

On the Tiles (pg. 135)—It will change into four triangle shapes.

A-Frame (page 136)—The design flip-flops. Take your pick!

Outlook (page 137)—Either is correct. The decision is yours.

Dotty (page 138–139)—You can see this any way you want.

Point the Way (page 140–141)—It depends on how you look at them. Both can be seen.

Which Way (page 142)—Either way. This is another design that flip-flops. Slowly bring the page close to your face, and then slowly take the page away from it. There you are—a painless extraction! (page 143)—Because this pattern can be viewed from either direction, the brain alternates from one view to the other.

High Side (page 144)—Another where the design flip-flops.

OP Tile (page 145)—You will probably see a small diamond shape in the center of the design surrounded by a bigger diamond shape.

Pieces of Eight (page 146)—The letters flip-flop so that we can see them pointing down to the left or up to the right.

The First Shall Be Last (page 147)—Turn the page upside down, and the word will change into "last."

IN YOUR FACE

Gram 'n' Gramp (page 150)—Both sets are the same, but lighter objects look bigger than darker ones.

Watch the Birdie (page 151)—The bird flies to the perch.

Bloomin' (page 152)—It looks like the one on the right, but they are both the same size. What tricks us is the petals around the center.

Little Goose Girl (page 153)—The girl feeds the goose.

Introvert/Extrovert (page 154–155)—Both circles are the same size. The arrows pull our eyes inward in the top circle, and our eyes follow the arrows outward in the lower one.

Beside Herself (page 156)—Bring the page close to your face. She will join up as if by magic!

Attention, Please! (page 157)—There are twelve letter **F**'s in the paragraph.

Noon (page 158)—It reads the same backward and forward. It also reads the same upside down.

Statue of Liberty (page 159)—It says "The Statue of of Liberty."

Hungry Snake (page 160)—Hold the page at eye level and slowly bring it toward your face. The snake swallows the bird.

Creepy (page 161)—It says, "Are you scared?"

Delusions (page 162)—The last word in every line appears twice.

Wake-Up Call (page 163)—The extra lines around the second clock create the illusion of movement.

Networking (page 164)—It flies into the net.

Fair and Square (page 165)—The three squares are identical. The ones with the vertical and horizontal lines in them just seem to occupy a larger area.

Squaring the Circle (page 166–167)—**A** looks a little larger than **B**, but both circles are the same size.

Stop or Go? (page 168)—In row **A** both circles are the same size, but the white one seems larger. When bright light falls on the retina of our eyes (where the nerve cells are), more nerve fibers react than actually had the light hit them. This causes a "spreading" effect, making the light object seem larger. In row **B** the black circle is actually larger, although both circles seem to be the same size.

Go for the Goal (page 169)—Yes, but they look different because of the way they have been placed in the angle.

Seeing Auras (page 170)—It's perfect.

Get Centered (page 171)—The one that is on the line, although it looks like the other one.

Mon Ami Pierrot (page 172)—You will see three hats and two stars.

Creel World (page 173)—You will see an extra rod. Sometimes you may see two extra rods. Amazing!

Aslant (page 174)—Use a ruler to line up the lines. Yes, it's **Y**.

Assignation (page 175)—The woman places the flower in the man's buttonhole.

John Marshall (page 176)—The left-hand door swung open leaving the right-hand side still in position. Cover the left-hand side of the door with a piece of blank paper, and read the new message.

You! (page 177)—It appears to follow you, but it's just an illusion.

Seeing Eye to Eye (page 178)—Your friend will appear to have one eye in the middle of his or her forehead.

Lovebirds (page 179)—The birds go into the cage.

VISUAL THINKING PUZZLES

What's Next? (page 182)—The next number is 10. The sequence is formed by first doubling a number and then subtracting 1.

Table for Two (page 183)—Oops! A knot will form in the spaghetti.

Galactica (page 184)—Block **F** is the correct answer. All five other blocks are identical, but block **F** is a mirror image of those blocks.

What's Your Sign? (page 185)—

$$5 \boxtimes 2 \boxminus 3 \boxplus 5 \boxdiv 4 = 3$$

Carny Load-Out (page 186)—

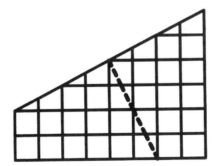

Rack 'em! (page 187)—Here are the diagrams for three new patterns.

The equal-side sums are **11**, **12**, and **9**, respectively.

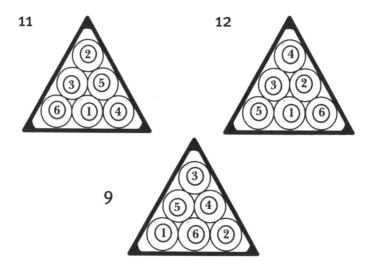

The Shadow Knows (page 188)—
It is a cylinder that has been cut into a wedge! Two slices that extend from the upper diameter to opposite sides of the bottom have been removed to form this shape.

Stop and Think (page 188–189)— There are eighteen paths. The easiest way to solve this puzzle is to start at the beginning and determine the number of paths that can get you to an intersection. The number of paths to each successive intersection is equal to the sum of the paths that are "attached" to it.

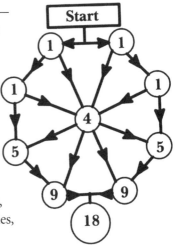

Equality Rules (page 190)— 27 triangles total: 16 one-cell triangles, 7 four-cell triangles, 3 nine-cell triangles, and one triangle with 16 cells.

Hidden in Plane Site (page 191)—The 15 squares include:

> One   4 x 4 square
> Two   3 x 3 squares
> Four 2 x 2 squares
> Eight 1 x 1 squares

More Joe (page 192)—Coffee pot **B** holds about four cups (half of pot **A**). The amount is determined by the height of the spout. The level cannot rise above the opening, because the extra coffee would spill out from the spout!

Gym Rat (page 193)—No, the belts are arranged in a pattern that doesn't allow them to move!

Profiling (page 194–195)—
C is the correct answer. The
cube that's not shown is shaded
in this diagram:

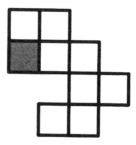

Link Latch (page 196)—Just open the bottom link! The top
two links are not attached to each other.

Amaze-ing String (page 197)—The string will come free of
the pipe. Start at the pipe to visualize this action. From there,
trace the pipe's path out from the center. After a few turns, the
pipe exits freely at the opening on the right side of the maze.

Pencil Stack (page 198)—Pencil #7

Naughty Notes (page 199)— G.

Reflecting Back (page 200–201)—

IV   III

Mirror Madness (page 202–203)— **A.**

Wrap It Up (page 204)—

Pharaoh Folds (page 205)—**B** is the only pattern that will produce a four-sided triangular pyramid.

Pi Pieces (page 206)—

Block Heads (page 207)—**E.**

On the March (page 208–209)—

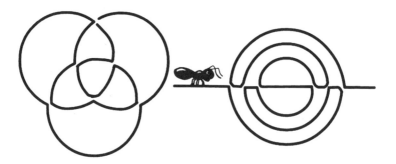

Roll With It (page 210)—**D.**

From Whence it Came? (page 211)—Pattern **D.**

HIDDEN PICTURES
HIDDEN FIGURES

Twinkle, Twinkle (page 215)—The star is center and at the very left edge of the picture.

Napoleon in Exile (page 216)—His head is shown by the **X**. See illustration at right.

Sweet Violets (page 217)—**X** marks their spot. See illustration at the left.

I'll Be Waiting (page 218)—Turn the picture upside down. You will see her head wearing a bonnet.

Schizoid (page 219)—There are two side profile faces looking at each other. When combined they form a third face that is looking straight ahead.

Optical Octagon
(page 220)—

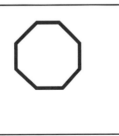

Crossed (page 221)—

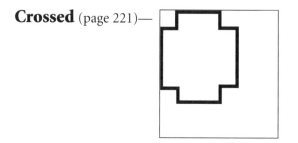

Chin Chin! (page 222)—Turn the page upside down. One of the boys is climbing on his beard.

Loving Cup (page 224)—It all depends on how you look at it.

Check. . . Mate (page 225)—Look carefully, and you will see two profile faces.

Dobbin (page 226)—A dog. Turn the page upside down. The dog can be seen tied up to a tree.

M' Lord (page 227)—Most people see the boy. You do not have to turn the page upside down to find the father. The boy's chin becomes the father's nose. It may help if you look at the page from a distance.

Daisy (page 228)—Turn the page upside down.

M' Lady (page 229)—The young lady's chin becomes the nose of the old lady. View the page from a distance.

Find the Missing Boats (page 230–231)—

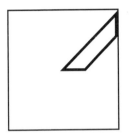 

Tumbling Cherubs (page 232)—Initially we see three. But since each head can join onto the different bodies, we get a grand total of seven. Can you work it out?

Vanity (page 233)—Viewed close up, it's a young lady looking at her reflection in a mirror. Viewed from a distance, it's a grinning skull.

Seeing Santa (page 234)—Turn the page so that the arrow points upward. Santa's face will be revealed.

Under the Mistletoe (page 235)—The face can belong to the man or the woman.

Kingdom Cow (page 236)—Look at the markings on the cow's back. You will see a map of the United Kingdom.

Tiger, Tiger (page 237)—Turn the page so that the arrows point upward. Look above the tiger's eyes, and you will see the kaiser looking to the left.

Hidden House (page 238)—

Octa-gone? (page 239)—

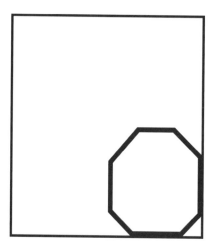

Old Mother Hubbard

(page 240–241)—Turn the book upside down, and you will see the landlord's face on the far left between the branches of the tree and the ground.

The butler's face is hidden in the dog's coat! If you turn the page upside down, you'll see that the dog's shoulder is also the butler's chin, and the butler's nose extends under the dog's arm.

One child's face is hidden in the top of Mother Hubbard's hat. Another is hidden upside down in the shoe, just above the tea tray. A third child's face can be seen below Mother Hubbard's shawl that wraps her shoulders, and a fourth bulges out of her apron, just below the bow tied around her waist. The last child is hidden in the hem of her apron!

There Be Giants (page 242)—Turn the page upside down. The two giants are looking down at the girl.

Foolish Love (page 243)—A clown wearing a three-pointed hat.

Strutting His Stuff (page 244)—He is found by turning the page upside down.

Old Stone-Face (page 245)—Turn the page 90° counter clockwise. His face will appear.

Spy Search (page 246)—Turn the page upside down. You will see his face formed from the branches between the trees.

Gossip (page 247)—You will see a grinning demon.

Pachyderm (page 248)—This elephant is made up entirely from the letters E L E P H A N T.

INDEX